7/14

Young Entrepreneurs

Run Your Own
Car Wash

Emma Carlson Berne

PowerKiDS press™

New York

Published in 2014 by The Rosen Publishing Group, Inc.
29 East 21st Street, New York, NY 10010

First Edition

Editor: Joanne Randolph
Book Design: Andrew Povolny
Photo Research: Katie Stryker

Photo Credits: Cover Marc Romanelli/Photographer's Choice/Getty Images; p. 4 Rob Marmion/Shutterstock.com; p. 5 jessica lewis/Flickr/Getty Images; pp. 7, 16 Jupiterimages/Creatas/Thinkstock; p. 8 Kraig Scarbinsky/Digital Vision/Getty Images; p. 9 rSnapshotPhotos/Shutterstock.com; p. 11 Naypong/Shutterstock.com; p. 12 Blend Images/ Shutterstock.com; p. 13 nicholas belton/E+/Getty Images; p. 14 Thomas Barwick/Iconica/ Getty Images; p. 17 J.D.S/Shutterstock.com; p. 18 Juanmonio/E+/Getty Images; p. 19 Poznyakov/Shutterstock.com; p. 21 John Panella/Shutterstock.com; p. 22 Pressmaster/ Shutterstock.com; p. 23 Fuse/Getty Images; p. 24 Thinkstock/Comstock/Thinkstock; p. 25 (top) isaravut/Shutterstock.com; p. 25 (bottom) Janis Smits/Shutterstock.com; p. 26 Gene Chutka/E+/Getty Images; p. 27 Istockphoto/Thinkstock; p. 28 Melissa Ross/Flickr/ Getty Images; p. 29 Innershadows Photography/Shutterstock.com.

Library of Congress Cataloging-in-Publication Data

Berne, Emma Carlson.
   Run your own car wash / by Emma Carlson Berne. — First edition.
      pages cm. — (Young entrepreneurs)
   Includes index.
   ISBN 978-1-4777-2920-5 (library) — ISBN 978-1-4777-3009-6 (pbk.) —
ISBN 978-1-4777-3080-5 (6-pack)
   1. Automobiles—Cleaning—Juvenile literature. 2. Car washes—Juvenile literature. 3. Money-making projects for children—Juvenile literature. I. Title.
   TL152.15.B47 2014
   629.28'7—dc23
                                        2013029470
Manufactured in the United States of America

CPSIA Compliance Information: Batch #W14PK2: For Further Information contact Rosen Publishing, New York, New York at 1-800-237-9932

Contents

"Hey, Kid, Want Some Money?"

"Mom, I need some more allowance! I don't have enough money." Does this sound like you? Actually, you might not need to ask your parents for money. If you are an organized, energetic person who likes to plan and **manage**, you might be a budding **entrepreneur**. An entrepreneur is someone who sees a need, creates a plan, and then organizes and manages a business to meet that need.

Instead of asking your mother for money, ask her to help you come up with ideas for how to make your own money.

Mowing lawns could be one business idea. Babysitting, dog walking, and selling lemonade are some other ways young people can make money.

Running your own business can be a lot of fun. It can also help people who need a product or service, and it can give you the spending money you need. Ready to get started?

Consider a Car Wash

All successful businesses supply a need or a want that people have. If your business doesn't provide a product or service that your customers desire, they won't **patronize** you. You must have customers to make money. Look around at your friends, parents, and neighbors. What sorts of goods and services do they use frequently?

In this book, we'll discuss how to run your own car wash. If you live in a community in which most people own cars, you have a built-in need. All cars eventually get dirty, and when they do, their owners will look around for a car wash. Then they'll see you!

Have you ever helped your father wash his car? Then you know just what supplies you need to start a car-washing business.

Think Hoses, Think Water

To run a successful car wash, you need to think things through and come up with a plan. Sit down with a notebook and write down three key questions: How will you run your car wash? Where will it be? When will you hold it?

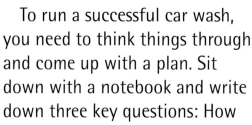

You can't have a car wash without water. You need to come up with a list of possible sites for your car wash based on whether they have a hose spigot you can use.

If you live in a house, your parents might be willing to let you hold your car wash in your driveway or on the street in front of your home.

For the "how" of your car wash, consider the key supplies you need to hold one. You need a driveway or parking lot with one or two hoses and **spigots** nearby. Thinking about this will also bring you to the question of where you will hold your car wash. Will you hold your car wash in your own driveway? Is there a school or a church parking lot that you can ask permission to use? Remember to pick a spot in which cars can easily pull in and out and that has room for cars to park while they are waiting for their turn.

Now think about when you will hold the car wash. You will want to hold your car wash when most people are home from work. A weekend is your best bet for having lots of cars available to come to your car wash. When scheduling, give yourself enough advance time to plan, buy supplies, and hire helpers, if necessary.

Tip Central

If you have to use a space you don't own, like a nearby parking lot, consider offering the owner of that parking lot a share of the **profits** in return for the loan of her property.

Write down your plan in a notebook. You can refer back to it as you get to each new step in your plan.

Budget, Budget, Budget

As a successful entrepreneur, one of the first things you will want to do is create a **budget**. A budget is a plan of how much money you will spend on your business and how much you expect to get out of it in profits. All businesses require some initial **investment** to begin. This is sometimes called start-up money.

Use the Internet to look up prices for some of the items you plan to use, then put those numbers in your budget. If you find that anything is more or less expensive when you actually buy it, be sure to adjust your budget.

As part of your budget, you will want to estimate how much money you could make. You will want to decide how much to charge your customers. Check the prices at a local car wash to get a sense of how much people will pay.

Tip Central

When budgeting for your car wash, don't forget to include less obvious expenses, like payment for helpers you might need, money for advertising, and tax on any purchases of items like buckets or soap.

WE NOW FEATURE! FULL SERVICE

CAR WASH

* CAR WASH
* MINI-VANS, JEEPS
  AND PICK-UPS

Polish Wax

Write down everything you think you might need to hold your car wash, including supplies, a water source, and **advertising**. Try to think through even the smallest details. Some of the things you need may not cost any money. Once you have your list completed, circle everything that you already own or can easily borrow and those that will not cost you anything.

Everything that is left, you will need to purchase. Look these items up on the Internet to get an idea of their costs. Then write an **estimate** of how much it will cost next to the item on your list. This is how much money you will be putting into your business.

Consider how many car washes you will have to provide at the price you have decided on to make that money back. Is that a realistic number? If not, you might have to reduce the amount or type of supplies you buy.

Expenses	
Advertising Supplies	$15.00
Car Wash Supplies	$25.00
Total	**$40.00**

Capital	
Savings	$35.00
Total	**$35.00**

Expenses – Capital = Total to Borrow
$40.00   – $35.00 = $5.00

Your budget should include the money you have to invest, and the money you need to spend. In this budget you need to borrow $5 from your parent or another person to cover your costs.

Add up your expenses using a calculator and write down the total. Do you have enough savings to cover your costs? If not, you may need to borrow money from your parents. Make a plan as to how and when you will pay them back.

Amazing Advertising

Have a friend hold up a sign at your car-wash site so customers know they have found the car wash.

No one will come to your car wash if they don't know where and when you are holding it. Like all businesses, you are going to need to advertise.

Tip Central

Consider donating a percentage of your profits to a charity or your school and mentioning that in your advertising. You might attract more customers since many people are happy to support a good cause.

Advertising does not just let your future customers know the basic details of your car wash. It should also inform them of any attractive discounts or specials you might be offering. You might make a sign advertising, "Cheapest car wash in town!" or "Come back with a second car, get half off your wash!"

Put a large sign at the corner of your street to help direct people to your car wash.

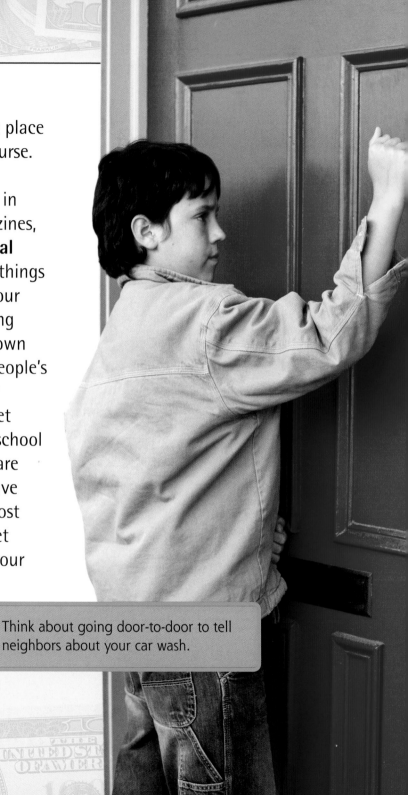

Advertising can take place in many **forums**, of course. There are TV and radio commercials, print ads in newspapers and magazines, and shout-outs in **social media**. Some of these things might cost a lot. For your budget, consider making signs to post around town and flyers to drop in people's mailboxes or hand out at school. Be sure to get permission from your school or city officials if you are posting signs. Some have rules about who can post and where. Don't forget to budget money for your advertising supplies.

Think about going door-to-door to tell neighbors about your car wash.

Poster board, markers, tape, printer paper, and ink are a few possible supplies you might need.

If your local newspaper has a section where you could post information about your car wash, think about posting something there. You could spend some money for an ad if it is not too expensive, or ask if you can list there for free.

Don't forget to include the cost of the supplies for your posters and signs in your budget.

Consider the nature of your business. Car washes take up a lot of room and require specific materials, such as hoses, water, and places for cars to park. You will have to think carefully about the site you choose. Make a list of all the locations nearby that have both water spigots where you can attach hoses and a large spot for the cars themselves. Consider your own driveway, your school parking lot, a church parking lot, or the parking lot of a store. Car washes create a lot of runoff, or soapy water that can harm plants. Will that be a problem at the site you choose?

If you can't hold a car wash at your house, maybe a local church will let you use their parking lot. You should plan to make a donation to the church and put it in your budget.

Talk to your friends about helping you with your car wash. Ask them to spread the word in their neighborhoods or apartment buildings, too.

Ask yourself if you will need helpers during your car wash. The people who work with you in your business are your human resources. If you choose to ask friends to help you, you should pay them either an hourly **wage** or a percentage of the profits.

A grocery store might let you use their parking lot for a car wash. Remind them that it could bring more customers into their store, too. If you can't use their lot, ask if you can hang a poster for your car wash on their community message board.

Tip Central

If you want to approach a storeowner for permission to use his parking lot for your car wash, point out that your car wash might bring in more customers for the store, too. People will stop to get their car washed and perhaps decide to do a little shopping also.

Well Supplied

It's time to gather your supplies. A few days in advance of your car wash, gather together the supplies you already have and put them in one spot, such as a corner of your garage.

Ask a parent to bring you to the hardware store or some other store where you can buy the items you circled on your list, such as buckets and large sponges.

A big bucket, dish soap, and a sponge are the basic supplies you need for your car wash.

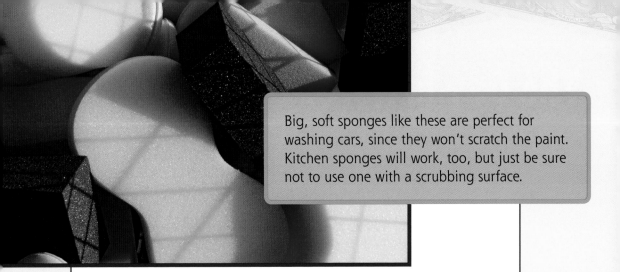

Big, soft sponges like these are perfect for washing cars, since they won't scratch the paint. Kitchen sponges will work, too, but just be sure not to use one with a scrubbing surface.

Save all your receipts so you know exactly how much each item cost. When you get home, put the purchases with your other supplies.

Then, total up the cost of all your purchases and write down the number. To make a profit, you will need to make more than you spent.

A squeegee, such as this, can be a helpful tool when washing cars. It helps clear extra water off windshields to avoid streaks or spots.

The Day Is Here!

On the big day, load the car for the ride to the wash site, or get busy at home. Hook up your hoses and organize your washing supplies neatly on a table. Hang a large sign with a catchy slogan and an arrow so people know where to pull in.

Here two girls have been given the job of standing by the road with signs. The rest of the team is washing cars.

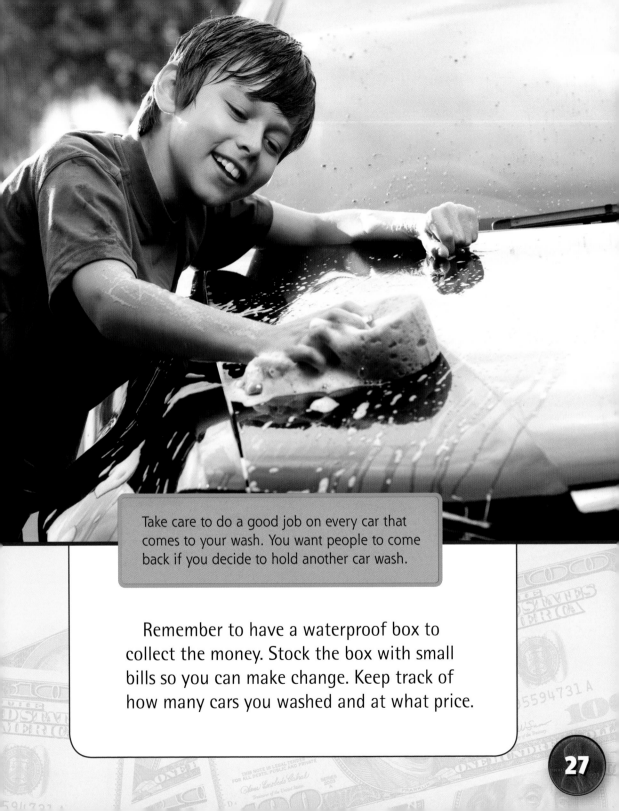

Take care to do a good job on every car that comes to your wash. You want people to come back if you decide to hold another car wash.

Remember to have a waterproof box to collect the money. Stock the box with small bills so you can make change. Keep track of how many cars you washed and at what price.

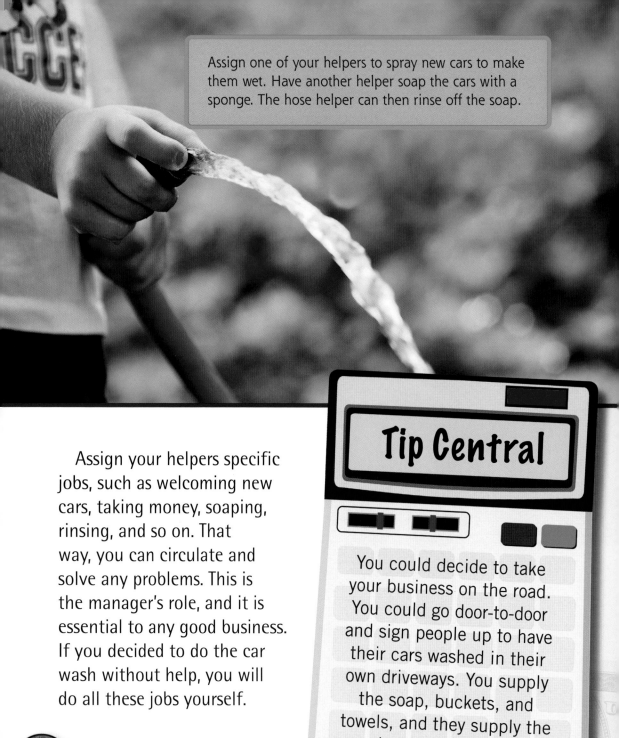

Assign one of your helpers to spray new cars to make them wet. Have another helper soap the cars with a sponge. The hose helper can then rinse off the soap.

Assign your helpers specific jobs, such as welcoming new cars, taking money, soaping, rinsing, and so on. That way, you can circulate and solve any problems. This is the manager's role, and it is essential to any good business. If you decided to do the car wash without help, you will do all these jobs yourself.

Tip Central

You could decide to take your business on the road. You could go door-to-door and sign people up to have their cars washed in their own driveways. You supply the soap, buckets, and towels, and they supply the hose and the car!

Either way, your car wash is going to be fun and successful if you have planned well.

At the end of the car wash, pay your helpers and clean up everything. Return any items you borrowed. Then add up the amount of money in the cash box and **reconcile** it with what you recorded during the wash.

Congratulations! Time to enjoy your profits.

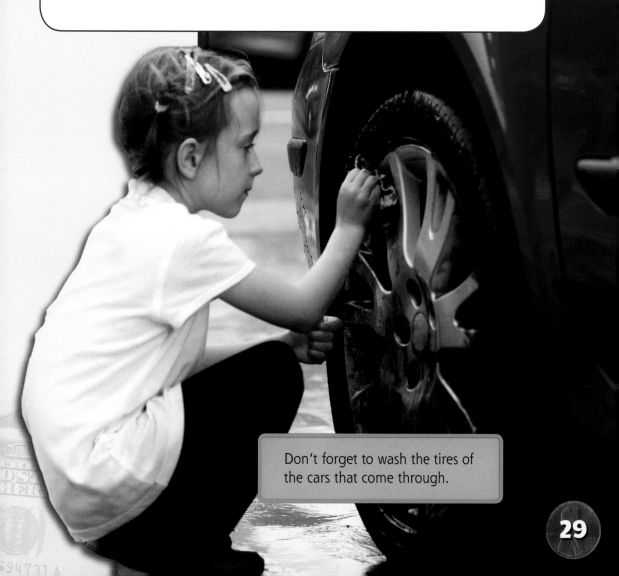

Don't forget to wash the tires of the cars that come through.

Are You Ready?

On a separate sheet of paper, check off these items to make sure you have everything ready for your car wash.

- [ ] Plan a day, time, and location for your car wash.
- [ ] Get permission to use any location that is not your home, like a store or church parking lot.
- [ ] Decide on a budget and make a "borrow" list and "buy" list.
- [ ] Buy supplies for advertising signs and flyers (for example poster board, thick markers, strong tape, colored paper, and extra printer ink).
- [ ] Make and distribute signs and flyers.
- [ ] Ask your friends to be helpers, and decide how much you will pay them.
- [ ] Gather "borrow" supplies and store them in one safe place. These might be hoses, a table, cash box, rags, and old towels for drying.
- [ ] Shop for "buy" supplies. These might include liquid soap and car polish or wax.
- [ ] Go to the bank or ask your parents for $1 and $5 bills for change.
- [ ] Organize supplies at your washing site, and hook up and test hoses.
- [ ] Hang up a sign at the washing site.
- [ ] Assign jobs to helpers.
- [ ] Smile and greet your customers!

Glossary

advertising (AD-vur-tyz-ing) Announcing something publicly, often to try to sell it.

budget (BUH-jit) A plan to spend a certain amount of money in a period of time.

entrepreneur (on-truh-pruh-NUR) A businessperson who has started his or her own business.

estimate (ES-teh-mayt) A guess based on knowledge or facts.

forums (FOR-umz) Places.

investment (in-VEST-ment) Putting money into things, such as a company, in the hope of getting more money later on.

manage (MA-nij) To conduct business.

patronize (PAY-truh-nyz) To be a regular customer of a business.

profits (PRAH-fits) The money a company makes after all its bills are paid.

reconcile (REH-kun-syl) To make sure one amount equals another amount.

social media (SOH-shul MEE-dee-uh) Online communities through which people share information, messages, photos, videos, and thoughts.

spigots (SPIH-gots) Faucets on the outsides of buildings where water comes out.

wage (WAYJ) The money that a person earns when he or she works.

Index

A

advertising,
14, 17–18

B

business(es), 4–6,
12, 15–16, 20,
22, 28

C

car(s), 6, 9–10, 17,
20, 26–28
cash box, 29–30
customers, 6,
17, 30

D

driveway(s),
9, 20

G

goods, 6

I

investment, 12

N

need, 4, 6

O

owner(s), 6

P

parking lot(s), 9,
20, 30
profit(s), 12, 22,
25, 29

S

service(s), 5–6
supplies, 9–10,
14–15, 18–19,
24–26, 30

W

wage, 22

Websites

Due to the changing nature of Internet links, PowerKids Press has developed an online list of websites related to the subject of this book. This site is updated regularly. Please use this link to access the list:
www.powerkidslinks.com/ye/car/